Gluten Free Treats Kids W

50 Delicious Gluten-Free

Sofia Davis

Just to say "Thank you" for purchasing this book, I'd like to give you a gift, absolutely free!

10 of the Best Paleo Smoothies eBook

Visit **seriouspaleo.com** now to download your free copy!

Disclaimer

Table of Contents

Introduction

More and more people nowadays get diagnosed with various forms of allergy or food intolerance and the gluten allergy is one of the most widespread worldwide. It isn't at all easy to cope with and gluten intolerance is not much better.

You might think that with the abundance of food in the world, finding gluten-free ingredients would be an easy task, but the truth is that a person suffering from this kind of allergy has to be very cautious when buying food. Unfortunately, if you have a gluten allergy you can't take the risk of buying ready-made food from the supermarket. Even eating at a restaurant can be tricky.

In these conditions, the only solution left is to cook at home. Home cooking has its advantages though, from being healthier to being able to control the flavors and ingredients and create recipes that fit your taste and likings. Plus, cooking is relaxing and rewarding in many ways, from the fulfillment you feel when you realize that you've make the food with your own hands to the delicious final product that will surely impress family and friends.

Home cooking also offers variety and since there aren't many gluten free desserts out there, ready to be bought and served, a cookbook focusing on the amazing world of desserts made with gluten free ingredients is more than welcomed.

Luckily, none of these recipes require any professional baking skills. Even if you've never baked before, these recipes will be a success simply because there is no room for going wrong: they are fail proof and the flavor combinations have been chosen so that the final results are delicious and luscious, rich and decadent while still being healthy and nutritious.

How do you do it? Buy the ingredients, choose a recipe and mix it up. That's all! Now wait for your dessert to bake into a decadent treat that will brighten up any dinner or meal and even find a place in your party buffets or special meals.

Ingredients and Equipment

Despite many beliefs, gluten free baking is easy if you have the best recipes and the right ingredients. You will require some special ingredients that have no gluten and are healthy and nutritious. Here is a list of all the main ingredients used in gluten-free baking.

Next time you go shopping consider stocking up on these, so you'll be covered whenever your sweet tooth goes crazy.

Agave syrup – also known as agave nectar, this sweetener is a great choice for substituting sugar in recipes, although sugar is gluten-free too. However, agave syrup is considered a healthier option. The agave nectar is made from the agave plant and it is similar to honey in terms of color and consistency. As a tip, when buying agave syrup, buy larger quantities because it ends up being cheaper. Plus, you will be using it quite a lot in baking and the last thing you want is to run out of it when you need it the most.

Almond flour – just like all-purpose flour, almond flour is very versatile and easy to use in both cooking and baking. When buying it, make sure it is fine and blanched, especially when you are buying it for desserts. I don't recommend buying large quantities of almond flour at once because it tends to attract butterflies and bugs. Buy what you need, plus a bit more, and store it in a dark and dry place, preferably not in an airtight container, but one that allows air to circulate and keep the flour dry. Almond flour is very similar to almond meal, except that the latter is slightly coarser. However, it can still be used in desserts with great success.

Coconut flour – if you are allergic to nuts as well, coconut flour is a great nut-free, gluten-free type of flour that can be easily used to create delicious, moist and flavorful desserts. Because it is lighter than almond flour, coconut flour is more suitable for cakes or cupcakes. But unlike other types of flour, it absorbs more liquid. If a recipe calls for 1 cup of almond flour, you can replace it with ¼ coconut flour.

Rice flour – another type of gluten-free flour that can be used in desserts is rice flour. It is made from finely milled rice and it comes in two varieties: white rice flour and brown rice flour. Both of them are easy to use and far more nutritious than wheat flour.

Arrowroot flour or powder – this ingredient has the same role as cornstarch in traditional recipes – it helps thicken liquids or makes batters lighter. It can be used in both savory cooking and sweet baking.

Cocoa powder – not only does cocoa powder taste great, it also has similar properties to regular flour, therefore many recipes call for less flour and more cocoa powder. That makes the final desserts lighter and gives them an intense flavor. I recommend using a raw type of cocoa powder because it preserves all the natural benefits of cocoa.

Dark chocolate – gluten-free dark chocolate is high in nutrients, mainly antioxidants, and can be used in desserts without worrying about weight gain for instance. Dark chocolate also has a lower sugar content which makes it even healthier. Not to mention that desserts made with chocolate are amazing, whether you are a chocoholic or not!

Vegetable oil – I generally use coconut oil when a recipe calls for vegetable oil just because it is healthy and has a lovely flavor, but sunflower, grape seed or other kinds of vegetable oil will work too as long as it doesn't have a strong distinctive flavor like olive oil has.

Baking powder and baking soda – when buying these two ingredients make sure they are gluten-free by reading the label. Sometimes certain additives are added, especially to baking powder, and they contain gluten, so better safe than sorry. Read the label carefully and choose the ones that clearly state that there is no gluten involved or there is no way that the product can be contaminated with gluten.

As for equipment and tools, gluten-free baking is no different from traditional baking. All you need is a few of the compulsory baking pans, a few bowls to mix batters, a mixer, a whisk and a few spoons or spatulas.

And don't forget about imagination and creativity in the kitchen! No recipe is set in stone and you are free to play with ingredients and customize recipes to fit your likings.

But most of all, enjoy the whole baking process and look at it as a way to relax rather than a chore. Only then you will obtain amazing results!

Recipes

Cakes

Chocolate Cake

This recipe is a classic and it had to be included in this book. Everyone loves it and it is such a versatile recipe. After all, chocolate pairs wonderfully with any other ingredient so feel free to add a few fresh or dried fruits into the batter too.

Prep time: 55 minutes
Servings: 12
Calories per serving: 311

Ingredients:
1 cup dates, pitted
½ cup butter, melted
¼ cup maple syrup
8oz dark chocolate, melted
5 eggs
1 teaspoon vanilla extract
1 cup almond flour
1 pinch salt
½ teaspoon baking soda
½ teaspoon baking powder
1 pinch nutmeg
¼ teaspoon cinnamon powder

Directions:
Mix the dates with the butter in a blender until smooth. Stir in the eggs and vanilla then add the melted chocolate and maple syrup. Fold in the almond flour, salt, baking powder, baking soda, nutmeg and cinnamon. Mix until well combined then pour the batter into a 9-icnh round cake pan and bake in the

preheated oven at 350F for 40-45 minutes. When the cake is done, let it cool in the pan then slice and serve either simple or topped with a dollop of whipped cream and a few fresh fruits, such as strawberries.

Flax Seed Chocolate Cake

Unlike the version above, this recipe contains no flour. The consistency of the cake is light and airy and the cake literally melts in your mouth bite after bite.

Prep time: 50 minutes
Servings: 8
Calories per serving: 291

Ingredients:
¼ cup flax seeds, ground
½ cup cold water
8 oz. dark chocolate, melted and chilled
¼ cup almond butter
1 egg
½ cup sugar
½ cup cocoa powder
1 pinch salt

Directions:
Mix the flax seeds with the water and let them soak for 10 minutes. Add the egg, chocolate and almond butter, as well as the sugar and mix very well. Fold in the cocoa powder and salt then spoon the batter into a small baking pan lined with parchment paper. Bake in the preheated oven at 350F for 40 minutes or until fragrant. When done, let the cake cool down then slice and serve.

Nociata Cake

Nociata is an Italian kind of cake that only uses walnuts and a sweetener as main ingredients. The final cake is similar to a large macaroon – moist on the inside and crisp on the outside and it is absolutely delicious.

Prep time: 20 minutes
Servings: 10
Calories per serving: 319

Ingredients:
2 cups maple syrup
2 cups walnuts, ground
1 pinch salt
1 pinch cinnamon powder

Directions:
Heat the maple syrup in a pan and place it over low to medium heat. Stir in the walnuts, salt and cinnamon and cook for 10 minutes, stirring all the time, making sure it doesn't stick to the bottom of the saucepan. Spoon the mixture into a small round cake pan lined with parchment paper and let it cool down and set. This cake doesn't require baking. When chilled, cut into slices and serve.

Gingerbread Cake

There's nothing more fragrant than this cake. It uses cinnamon powder, ginger, cloves and a touch of nutmeg to spice it all up. The rich batter yields a delicious cake that can easily sit on your festive table.

Prep time: 1 hour
Servings: 10
Calories per serving: 245

Ingredients:
1 cup sorghum flour
1 cup almond flour
½ cup potato cornstarch
1 cup brown sugar
1 teaspoon baking powder
1 teaspoon cinnamon powder
½ teaspoon ground ginger
½ teaspoon ground cloves
1 pinch nutmeg
1 pinch salt
1 tablespoon cocoa powder
2 eggs
¼ cup almond milk
1 teaspoon vanilla extract
4 tablespoons vegetable oil

Directions:
In a bowl, mix the flours with the cornstarch, sugar, baking powder, spices, salt and cocoa powder. Stir in the eggs, almond milk, vanilla and oil and give it a good mix until well combined and smooth. Pour the batter in a 9-inch cake pan lined with parchment paper. Bake in the preheated oven at 350F for 40-50 minutes. To check for doneness, insert a toothpick in

the center of the cake. If it comes out clean, the cake is done. If the toothpick had traces of batter, the cake needs a few more minutes of baking. When done, remove the pan from the oven and let the cake cool in the pan. Sprinkle with powdered sugar and serve.

Beet Chocolate Cake

The earthy flavor of the beets works great with the bittersweet chocolate and not only that it adds a subtle flavor, but it also preserves the cake moist for a longer period of time, making it fudgy and delicious. Who knew that such a common vegetable could taste so good in desserts?!

Prep time: 50 minutes
Servings: 6
Calories per serving: 170

Ingredients:
1 ripe banana, mashed
2/3 cup cocoa powder
½ teaspoon baking soda
½ teaspoon baking powder
1 pinch salt
1 small beet, blended
¼ cup agave syrup
4 tablespoons vegetable oil
1 teaspoon vanilla extract

Directions:
Mix the mashed banana with the blended beet, oil, agave syrup and vanilla. Stir in the cocoa powder, baking powder, baking soda and a pinch of salt. Pour the batter into a small baking pan lined with parchment paper and bake in the preheated oven at 350F for 40 minutes. When done, remove the pan from the oven and let the cake cool down in the pan. Top with a bit of cocoa powder, slice and serve.

Blueberry Polenta Cake

Polenta flour is a great choice of a gluten free flour substitute because it is easy to find and it also has a mild distinctive taste. In this particular recipe, the polenta is combined with blueberries and lemon zest to create a cake that is rather dense, but fragrant and delicious.

Prep time: 1 hour
Servings: 14
Calories per serving: 309

Ingredients:
Cake:
1 cup butter, room temperature
1 cup sugar
1 cup almond flour
1 cup polenta flour
3 eggs
1 cup fresh or frozen blueberries
1 pinch salt
1 tablespoon lemon zest
Glaze:
1 ¼ cups powdered sugar
2 tablespoons lemon juice
1 tablespoon lemon zest

Directions:
To make the cake, combine the butter and sugar in a bowl and mix until smooth and creamy
. Stir in the eggs and lemon zest then fold in the almond flour and polenta flour. Fold in the blueberries then pour the batter into a small round cake pan lined with parchment paper. Bake in the preheated oven at

350F for 45 minutes then remove from heat and let it cool down slightly then transfer on a serving platter.
For the glaze, mix all the ingredients in a bowl then drizzle it over the cake. Let it set 1 hour then slice and serve.

Hazelnut Chocolate Cake

The hazelnuts and the chocolate create one of the best cakes you will ever have. Imagine a chocolate hazelnut bar, but in the form of a cake, a bit more fluffy, but just as fudgy and delicious. Chocoholic or not, you will fall in love with this recipe.

Prep time: 8
Servings: 10
Calories per serving: 374

Ingredients:
6 oz. dark chocolate (at least 85% cocoa content), melted
½ cup butter, softened
6 eggs
¼ cup sugar
1 ½ cups ground hazelnuts
1 pinch salt

Directions:
Mix the eggs with the sugar and salt until they double their volume then stir in the soft butter, followed by the melted chocolate. Fold in the ground hazelnuts and spoon the batter into a round cake pan lined with parchment paper. Bake in the preheated oven at 350F for 40-45 minutes or until fragrant. When done, remove the cake from the oven and let it cool down before slicing and serving.

Orange Crepe Cake

So many layers of crepes and orange buttercream! Imagine the delicate crepes and the soft, silky and fragrant buttercream melting in your mouth bite after bite. This cake might take some time to make, but the final result is truly impressive and it's well worth it.

Prep time: 1 hour
Servings: 16
Calories per serving: 347

Ingredients:
Crepes:
4 eggs
¼ cup butter, melted
3 cups milk
2 cups rice flour
1 cup potato cornstarch
½ cup tapioca flour
1 pinch salt
Orange buttercream:
1 cup butter, room temperature
2 cups powdered sugar
1 cup orange juice
4 teaspoons orange zest
2 tablespoons Grand Marnier

Directions:
To make the crepes, combine all the ingredients in a bowl or even a blender and mix very well until smooth and perfectly combined. Let the batter rest for 30 minutes.
Heat a crepe pan over medium heat and brush it slightly with vegetable oil. Pour a few tablespoons of batter into the pan and move it around to evenly coat

its bottom. Fry the crepe on one side for 1 minute then flip it over and finish frying until golden brown. Transfer it on a platter and repeat with the remaining batter.

To make the buttercream, mix the butter with an electric mixer or stand mixer until creamy then add the sugar and keep mixing at least 5 minutes, gradually adding the orange juice, orange zest and Grand Marnier.

To finish the cake, spread a bit of buttercream on each crepe and layer them one over another on a platter. Cover with buttercream and decorate as you like. Let it rest a few hours then cut and serve.

Quinoa Cranberry Cake

This cake uses quinoa cake in a successful attempt of making desserts healthier. The final taste is rich and flavorful though and the cake is moist, loaded with nutrients that will boost your digestion and keep you full for a longer time. As you can see, this is more than just a dessert.

Prep time: 50 minutes
Servings: 8
Calories per serving: 167

Ingredients:
1 cup quinoa flakes
1 cup rolled oats, ground
¼ cup flax seeds, ground
1 teaspoon baking powder
½ teaspoon baking soda
1 pinch salt
¼ cup agave syrup
2 eggs
2 tablespoons orange zest
¼ cup orange juice
½ cup dried cranberries

Directions:
Mix the quinoa flakes, oats, flax seeds, baking powder, baking soda and salt in a bowl. Stir in the eggs, agave syrup, orange zest and orange juice then fold in the cranberries. Pour the batter into a small baking pan lined with parchment paper and bake in the preheated oven at 350F for 30-40 minutes or until golden brown and fragrant. When done, remove from heat and set aside to cool down before slicing and serving. If you want, you can make an orange glaze

from powdered sugar and orange juice until it reaches the consistency you like then drizzle it over the cake.

Lime and Coconut Cake

This cake redefines the word fresh when it comes to cakes. The delicate flavor of the coconut and the intense aroma of the lime balance each other perfectly and manage to create a cake that can get addictive due to its amazing flavor and moist inside.

Prep time: 50 minutes
Servings: 12
Calories per serving: 339

Ingredients:
Cake:
1 cup soy flour
½ cup almond flour
½ cup shredded coconut
1 pinch salt
1 teaspoon baking soda
1 cup sugar
4 eggs
½ cup butter, room temperature
2 limes, juiced and zested
Frosting:
2/3 cup cream cheese
¼ cup butter, softened
1 cup powdered sugar
1 teaspoon lime zest
½ teaspoon vanilla extract

Directions:
In a bowl, mix the butter with the sugar until creamy and smooth. Add the lime juice and zest, as well as the zest then incorporate the dry ingredients. Mix very well and spoon the batter into a small round cake pan lined with parchment paper. Bake the cake in the hot

oven at 350F for 40 minutes or until the cake starts to turn golden brown and fragrant. When done, remove the cake from the oven and let it cool down.

To make the frosting, mix the cream cheese with the butter until creamy then add the powdered sugar, vanilla and lime zest. Spread the frosting over the cake and decorate with coconut flakes.

Muffins and Cupcakes

Quinoa Chocolate Muffins

Quinoa is such a versatile ingredient. It can easily be used in savory foods, but also in desserts and these muffins are a great option to try it out. They are moist and pack a lot of flavor and deliciousness.

Prep time: 35 minutes
Servings: 12
Calories per serving: 175

Ingredients:
3 ripe bananas, mashed
½ cup coconut milk
2 tablespoons vegetable oil
1 teaspoon vanilla extract
½ cup sugar
1 cup quinoa flakes
½ cup cocoa powder
1 teaspoon baking powder
1 pinch salt
½ cup walnuts, chopped

Directions:
Mix the mashed bananas with the coconut milk, oil, vanilla and sugar. Stir in the quinoa, cocoa powder, salt and baking powder then fold in the chopped walnuts. Spoon the batter into 12 muffin cups lined with muffin papers and bake in the hot oven at 350F for 20-25 minutes or until golden brown and fragrant. Let them cool in the pan before serving.

Strawberry Cream Cheese Cupcakes

These cupcakes are so fresh and delicious that you will surely be making them again and again. The cream cheese topping is absolutely delicious and so versatile that you can replace the strawberries with any other fruits you want, creating a whole new recipe.

Prep time: 40 minutes
Servings: 12
Calories per serving: 296

Ingredients:
Cupcakes:
1 ½ cups rice flour
1 teaspoon baking powder
1 pinch salt
1 pinch cinnamon powder
½ cup sugar
2 eggs
½ cup Greek style yogurt
¼ cup milk
1 teaspoon vanilla extract
1 cup strawberries, chopped
Frosting:
8 oz. cream cheese, room temperature
½ cup butter, softened
1 cup powdered sugar
¼ cup strawberries, pureed
1 teaspoon vanilla extract

Directions:
To make the cupcakes, mix the rice flour with the baking powder, salt and cinnamon powder. Add the sugar then stir in the eggs, yogurt, milk and vanilla. Mix very well then fold in the chopped strawberries.

Spoon the batter into 12 muffin cups lined with muffin papers and bake in the preheated oven at 350F for 20-30 minutes or until golden brown and fragrant. When done, remove from the oven and let them cool in the pan.

To make the frosting, mix the butter with the cream cheese until creamy and fluffy then stir in the powdered sugar and mix until creamy. Stir in the strawberry puree and vanilla then spoon the cream into a pastry bag and decorate the cupcakes.

Peanut Butter Muffins

Everyone loves peanut butter and luckily it can be used in desserts too, infusing them with its amazing taste and flavor and making them rich, moist and delicious.

Prep time: 35 minutes
Servings: 10
Calories per serving: 189

Ingredients:
¼ cup flax seeds, ground
½ cup peanut butter
1 cup applesauce
¼ cup agave syrup
1 teaspoon vanilla extract
1 teaspoon baking soda
1 pinch salt
1 cup rice flour

Directions:
Mix the flax seeds with the applesauce then stir in the agave syrup and peanut butter, as well as the vanilla. Fold in the rice flour, salt and baking soda then spoon the batter into your muffin cups, preferably lined with muffin papers. Bake in the preheated oven at 350F for 20-25 minutes or until golden brown. Let them cool in the pan before serving.

Chocolate Chip Muffins

Crumbly and delicious, these muffins will surely impress any eaters. The chocolate chips add such a nice texture and once you bite into one of these muffins, you will want more and more. Serve them with a cup of warm milk and you've got yourself a delicious sweet snack.

Prep time: 30 minutes
Servings: 12
Calories per serving: 166

Ingredients:
1 cup plain yogurt
½ cup applesauce
½ cup sugar
1 pinch salt
1 teaspoon baking powder
½ cup potato cornstarch
1 cup rice flour
1 cup dark chocolate chips (85% cocoa)

Directions:
In a bowl, mix the plain yogurt with the applesauce, sugar and salt. Stir in the cornstarch, rice flour, and baking powder then mix very well. Fold in the chocolate chips then spoon the batter into your muffin cups and bake in the hot oven at 350F for 25 minutes or until golden brown. Let them cool in the pan before serving.

Banana Chocolate Muffins

Combining bananas with chocolate is an all-time classic and it works every single time, whether it is a cake or these moist and delicious muffins. Adding a few chunks of bananas into the batter boost the flavor and gives them even more moisture.

Prep time: 35 minutes
Servings: 12
Calories per serving: 146

Ingredients:
1 cup rice flour
¼ cup potato starch
1 teaspoon baking powder
1 pinch salt
¼ cup cocoa powder
2 eggs
¼ cup sugar
2 ripe bananas, mashed
1 ripe banana, chopped
4 tablespoons vegetable oil
1 teaspoon vanilla extract

Directions:
In a bowl, mix the rice flour with the cornstarch, baking powder, salt and cocoa powder. In a different bowl, combine the eggs with the sugar until creamy. Stir in the mashed bananas, vegetable oil and vanilla extract. Fold in the banana chunks then spoon the batter into your muffin cups and bake in the preheated oven at 350F for 25 minutes or until golden brown and fragrant. Let them cool in the pan before serving.

Lemon Chia Seed Muffins

Similar to poppy seed muffins, these delightful sweets are fragrant and healthy, loaded with nutrients and a real treat for your taste buds. Each bite gives you an interesting flavor contrast between the tangy lemon batter and the crunchy, rich chia seeds.

Prep time: 35 minutes
Servings: 12
Calories per serving: 170

Ingredients:
½ cup coconut flour
½ cup rice flour
1 teaspoon baking soda
1 pinch salt
2 tablespoons coconut oil
½ cup coconut milk
4 eggs
¼ cup agave syrup
1 tablespoon lemon zest
2 tablespoons lemon juice
1 teaspoon vanilla extract
3 tablespoons chia seeds

Directions:
Mix the coconut flour with the rice flour, baking soda and salt. Stir in the coconut milk, eggs, agave syrup, lemon zest, lemon juice and vanilla extract. Fold in the chia seeds then spoon the batter into your muffin cups lined with parchment paper. Bake the muffins in the preheated oven at 350F for 20-25 minutes or until well risen and fragrant. When done, remove them from the oven and let them cool in the pan before serving.

Coconut and Goji Berry Muffins

These coconut muffins are delicate and will surely be a delight for your taste buds, while the Goji berries boost their nutritional content by adding plenty of antioxidants and fibers.

Prep time: 40 minutes
Servings: 10
Calories per serving: 199

Ingredients:
1 cup buckwheat flour
½ cup almond flour
1 teaspoon baking powder
¼ cup cocoa powder
1 pinch cinnamon powder
1 pinch salt
1 cup coconut milk
2 tablespoons vegetable oil
1 teaspoon vanilla extract
¼ cup agave syrup
¼ cup Goji berries, chopped
¼ cup coconut flakes

Directions:
Mix the buckwheat flour with the almond flour, baking powder, cocoa powder and salt. Stir in the coconut milk, oil, vanilla extract and agave syrup and give it a good mix. Fold in the Goji berries and coconut flakes then spoon the batter into your muffin cups lined with special muffin papers. Bake in the preheated oven at 350F for 20-25 minutes or until golden brown and fragrant. Let them cool in the pan before serving them.

Apple Walnut Cupcakes

I love it when simple ingredients like apples can turn an otherwise common dessert into something amazing, like these fragrant and rich cupcakes with a moist and fragrant inside.

Prep time: 1 hour
Servings: 16
Calories per serving: 346

Ingredients:
Cupcakes:
2 green apples, diced
1 teaspoon cinnamon powder
2 eggs
¼ cup vegetable oil
½ cup agave syrup
1 teaspoon vanilla extract
1 cup cashew nuts, ground
1 ½ cups ground flax seeds
1 teaspoon baking soda
1 pinch salt
½ cup walnuts, chopped
Frosting:
½ cup butter
1 cup cream cheese
4 tablespoons maple syrup
¼ cup powdered sugar

Directions:
Combine the eggs with the oil, agave syrup and vanilla extract. Stir in the ground cashews, flax seeds, baking soda and salt then fold in the diced apples, cinnamon and walnuts. Spoon the batter into your muffin cups lined with special muffin papers and bake in the

preheated oven at 350F for 20-25 minutes or until golden brown and fragrant. Let them cool in the pan before transferring on a serving platter.

To make the frosting, mix the butter with the cream cheese until creamy. Stir in the maple syrup and powdered sugar then spoon the frosting over each cupcake. Serve them right away.

Blueberry Cupcakes

Blueberries are so delicate and so are these cupcakes. The batter is flavorful and rich in fibers and proteins, but that only gives them an emphasized taste and makes them a healthy dessert to indulge on whenever your sweet tooth goes crazy.

Prep time: 1 hour
Servings: 14
Calories per serving: 360

Ingredients:
Cupcake:
1 cup almond flour
½ cup rice flour
½ cup potato starch
1 teaspoon baking powder
1 pinch salt
1 cup sugar
4 tablespoons vegetable oil
1 teaspoon vanilla extract
1 cup almond milk
1 egg
½ cup blueberries
Frosting:
½ cup butter, softened
2 cups powdered sugar
1 teaspoon vanilla extract
2 tablespoons almond milk

Directions:
To make the cupcakes, mix the almond flour with the rice flour, potato starch, baking powder, salt and sugar in a bowl. Stir in the vegetable oil, vanilla, almond milk and egg then fold in the blueberries. Spoon the batter

into your muffin cups lined with parchment paper and bake in the preheated oven at 350F for 25 minutes or until golden brown. Let them cool down in the pan.

For the frosting, mix the butter until creamy then gradually add the powdered sugar, vanilla and finally the almond milk. Mix for 5 minutes until fluffy then spoon the cream in a pastry bag and pipe it on your cupcakes. Serve them fresh.

Mocha Cupcakes

These chocolate and coffee cupcakes are the perfect way to start your mornings. With a cup of coffee and a cupcakes your day will surely be amazing and joyful.

Prep time: 1 hour
Servings: 14
Calories per serving: 316

Ingredients:
Cupcakes:
1 cup rice flour
1 cup almond flour
1 cup sugar
½ cup cocoa powder
1 teaspoon baking powder
1 pinch salt
3 eggs
½ cup vegetable oil
¾ cup hot water
2 teaspoons instant coffee
Frosting:
2 cups heavy cream
2 tablespoons powdered sugar
1 teaspoon vanilla extract
2 oz. dark chocolate, melted

Directions:
To make the cupcakes, mix the rice flour with the almond flour, sugar, cocoa, baking powder and salt. In a different bowl, combine the eggs with the oil, hot water and instant coffee then pour this mixture over the dry ingredients. Give it a good mix then spoon the batter into your muffin cups lined with muffin papers.

Bake in the preheated oven at 350F for 20-25 minutes or until fragrant. Let them cool in the pan.

For the frosting, whip the heavy cream with the powdered sugar and stir in the vanilla. Spoon the whipped cream in your pastry bag and decorate the cupcakes. Serve them fresh.

Cookies

Black and White Sesame Seed Cookies

Sesame seeds are not only highly fragrant, but also rich in nutrients, such as good fats and fibers. And because they come in two varieties, black and white, why not use both to create a contrasting cookie that tastes amazing.

Prep time: 1 hour
Servings: 2 dozen
Calories per serving: 157

Ingredients:
1 cup butter, cubed
1 cup almond flour
½ cup coconut flour
1/3 cup sugar
1 pinch salt
1 egg
1 egg yolk
2 tablespoons black sesame seeds
3 tablespoons white sesame seed cookies

Directions:
Mix the butter with the sugar until creamy then add the egg and egg yolks. Stir in the almond flour and coconut flour, as well as the salt and sesame seeds. Mix well then form a log and wrap it well in plastic wrap. Freeze the dough for 30 minutes then cut into ¼-inch thick slices and place them all on a baking tray with the cut facing up. Bake the cookies at 350F for 20 minutes or until the edges begin to brown. Let them

cool in the pan then store them in an airtight container before serving.

Coconut Chocolate Chip Cookies

These cookies are buttery, crumbly and delicate due to the coconut, while the dark chocolate chips add a bittersweet taste that balances everything perfectly by creating a delightful contrast for your taste buds.

Prep time: 40 minutes
Servings: 1 dozen
Calories per serving: 193

Ingredients:
½ cup coconut oil
½ cup sugar
1 cup shredded coconut
2 tablespoons coconut flour
1 pinch salt
½ teaspoon baking soda
1 teaspoon lemon zest
2 eggs
¼ cup dark chocolate chips

Directions:
Mix the coconut oil with the sugar, lemon zest and eggs. Stir in the coconut, salt, baking soda and coconut flour then fold in the dark chocolate chips. Drop spoonfuls of batter on a baking tray lined with parchment paper and bake in the hot oven at 350F for 20-25 minutes or until golden brown and fragrant. Store them in an airtight container when chilled.

Chocolate Pistachio Cookies

Although the combination between chocolate and pistachio is not very common, they do work together, creating some rich, luscious cookies that can surely become addictive. They are moist on the inside and chewy on the outside, the perfect mix between the bitterness of the chocolate and the earthy flavor of the pistachio.

Prep time: 40 minutes
Servings: 2 dozen
Calories per serving: 95

Ingredients:
2 cups powdered sugar
1 pinch salt
1 cup cocoa powder
4 egg whites
1 cup pistachio, finely chopped

Directions:
Quickly mix the egg whites with the sugar, salt and cocoa powder in a bowl. Stir in the pistachio then drop spoonfuls of batter on a cookie tray lined with parchment paper. Bake in the preheated oven at 350F for 20-25 minutes or until crusty on the outside. Let them cool in the pan before serving. Store the cookies in an airtight container to preserve their taste.

Chestnut Cookies

The thing with chestnuts is that you either love them or hate them, but for those of you who love them, here is a recipe that brings out the most of chestnuts. Their flavor is intense and the texture is delightful.

Prep time: 1 hour
Servings: 2 dozen
Calories per serving: 99

Ingredients:
1 cup almond flour
¼ cup potato starch
¼ cup coconut flour
¼ cup cocoa powder
1 pinch salt
2 eggs
¼ cup butter, melted
¼ cup agave syrup
¼ cup chestnut puree

Directions:
In a bowl, mix the eggs with the butter, agave syrup and chestnut puree then stir in the almond flour, potato starch, cocoa powder and a pinch of salt. Drop spoonfuls of batter on a prepared cookie tray and bake in the preheated oven at 350F for 20-25 minutes or until fragrant. Let them cool in the pan before storing in an airtight container or cookie jar.

Double Chocolate Cookies

Chocoholic all over the world, this recipe is for you! These cookies have so much chocolate and the taste is so intense that you won't be able to stop at just a few cookies. The recipe can surely get addictive.

Prep time: 40 minutes
Servings: 2 dozen
Calories per serving: 155

Ingredients:
½ cup cocoa powder
½ cup flax seeds, ground
½ cup potato starch
1 pinch salt
1 ½ cups black beans, drained
¼ cup vegetable oil
½ cup agave syrup
½ cup dark chocolate chips

Directions:
In a blender, mix the beans with the agave syrup, vegetable oil and salt until smooth. Stir in the remaining ingredients then drop spoonfuls of batter on a baking tray lined with parchment paper. Bake them in the preheated oven at 350F for 20-25 minutes or until fragrant and crusty. Let them cool in the pan before transferring in a sealed cookies jar to store.

Yogurt and Coconut Cookies

These cookies are so delicate, chewy and moist. The yogurt sure adds an interesting flavor that combines perfectly with the coconut flakes. Use a full fat yogurt because it will add more flavor and make the cookies moister, as well as help preserving them fresh for a longer time.

Prep time: 50 minutes
Servings: 3 dozen
Calories per serving: 80

Ingredients:
½ cup butter, softened
2/3 cup brown sugar
1 egg
½ cup Greek style yogurt
1 teaspoon vanilla extract
1 cup rice flour
1 pinch salt
1 teaspoon baking soda
½ teaspoon baking powder
1 ½ cups shredded coconut

Directions:
Mix the butter with the brown sugar until creamy and fluffy then stir in the egg, vanilla extract and yogurt. Add the flour, baking soda, baking powder, salt and shredded coconut and mix well. Drop spoonfuls of dough on a prepared baking tray and bake in the preheated oven at 350F for 20-25 minutes or until the edges turn golden brown and crisp. Let the cookies cool in the pan and store them in a sealed cookie jar.

Almond Cookies

With just a few ingredients, this recipe manages to create some crumbly, delicate and delicious cookies that can become a nice afternoon snack as well, next to a cup of tea or a glass of warm milk.

Prep time: 35 minutes
Servings: 2 dozen
Calories per serving: 115

Ingredients:
2 cups almond flour
½ cup almond milk
¼ cup agave syrup
¼ cup vegetable oil
1 pinch salt
½ teaspoon baking powder

Directions:
Combine all the ingredients in a food processor and pulse until well mixed. Drop spoonfuls of batter on a cookie tray lined with baking paper. Bake them in the hot oven at 350F for 20 minutes until the edges are just slightly golden brown. When done, remove them from the oven and let them cool in the pan before storing them in a sealed cookie jar.

Vanilla Meringues

Meringues must be some of the easiest treats ever. They only require 2 main ingredients and you don't need any special skills to make them. Don't mind the myths that have been going around about meringues because they are easier than you think. The baking time is indeed longer, but you can just forget about them in the oven for a while. If the temperature is right, they won't burn.

Prep time: 2 hours
Servings: 4 dozen
Calories per serving: 14

Ingredients:
4 egg whites
1 pinch salt
½ cup sugar
4 tablespoons powdered sugar
1 teaspoon vanilla extract
Seeds from 1 vanilla bean

Directions:
Mix the egg whites with the salt until salty then gradually stir in the sugar, mixing at least 5 more minutes. Add the powdered sugar and continue mixing until glossy and stiff. Stir in the vanilla extract and vanilla seeds then spoon the mixture into a pastry bag. Pipe small meringues onto a cookie sheet lined with parchment paper. If you don't have a pastry bag, don't worry. You can simply drop spoonfuls of mixture on the sheet. They will look more rustic, but still taste great. Bake them in the preheated oven at 300F for about 2 hours. The reason the temperature is so low is

that they need to dry rather than bake and turn golden brown.

Date and Banana Cookies

With just five ingredients, this recipe manages to create some healthy and nutritious cookies that can be either a rich dessert or a nourishing snack in the afternoon. The recipe itself is very fragrant and versatile.

Prep time: 30 minutes
Servings: 2 dozen
Calories per serving: 84

Ingredients:
1 cup dates, pitted
1 ripe banana, mashed
2 tablespoons vegetable oil
1 cup almond flour
½ cup rolled oats
1 pinch salt

Directions:
Mix the dates with the banana and oil in a food processor and pulse until well blended. Stir in the almond flour and rolled oats. Add a pinch of salt and mix well with a spatula. Drop spoonfuls of batter on a cookie tray lined with baking paper and bake in the preheated oven at 350F for 20 minutes or until the cookies begin to turn golden brown and fragrant. Cool them completely before transferring in a sealed cookie jar.

Spiced Biscotti

Biscotti is the Italian term for cookies or biscuits. However, the way biscotti are made is different from the cookies you know, mainly because biscotti are baked until dry and that makes them perfect for being served next to a cup of tea or coffee.

Prep time: 50 minutes
Servings: 2 dozen
Calories per serving: 107

Ingredients:
1 cup brown rice flour
½ cup almond flour
½ cup coconut flour
1 teaspoon baking powder
1 pinch salt
1 teaspoon cinnamon powder
½ teaspoon ground ginger
½ teaspoon ground cloves
¼ cup vegetable oil
1 egg
4 tablespoons maple syrup
½ cup hazelnuts

Directions:
In a bowl, mix the flours with the baking powder, salt and spices. Stir in the egg, oil and maple syrup then fold in the hazelnuts. Transfer the dough on a baking tray and shape it into a log. Bake in the preheated oven at 350F for 20 minutes then remove from the oven and cut in ½-inch thick slices. Place the slices back on the tray with the cut facing up and continue baking them for 15 more minutes. Let them cool in the pan before serving or storing them.

Fruit Desserts

Blueberry Pudding Cake

A moist and delicious cake that takes advantage of the lovely flavor of blueberries. The final texture is pudding-like, therefore delicious and amazing served with a scoop of ice cream or a dollop of heavy cream.

Prep time: 50 minutes
Servings: 10
Calories per serving: 168

Ingredients:
1 cup almond meal
½ cup rice flour
1 teaspoon baking powder
1 pinch salt
½ cup almond milk
¼ cup agave syrup
4 egg whites
4 cups blackberries, fresh or frozen

Directions:
Place the blueberries in a deep dish baking pan and set aside.
In a bowl, mix the almond meal, rice flour, baking powder and salt. Stir in the rest of the ingredients then pour the batter over the fruits. Bake in the preheated oven at 350F for 40 minutes or until golden brown and fragrant. Serve warm with ice cream or chilled with whipped cream.

Strawberry Panna Cotta

Panna cotta is an Italian pudding like dessert, delicious and very versatile. This recipe uses strawberries to flavor it, but you can use any other fruit you like or even replace the fruits with chocolate, coffee or simply vanilla.

Prep time: 25 minutes
Servings: 6
Calories per serving: 374

Ingredients:
3 cups almond milk
½ cup heavy cream
1 cup strawberries, pureed
¼ cup agave syrup
1 teaspoon vanilla extract
3 teaspoons gelatin
¼ cup cold water

Directions:
Mix the cold water with the gelatin and set aside to soak.
Combine the almond milk with the agave syrup and heavy cream and heat them up slightly on low heat. Stir in the strawberry puree and vanilla then add the bloomed gelatin. Mix well until dissolved then pour the panna cotta into small individual servings and refrigerate at least 1 hour before serving it.

Walnut Baked Apples

Baked apples are delicious even simple, but imagine adding a bit of crunch with this rich and flavorful filling. The recipe is a n easy one nonetheless and it can be done at any time of the year because apples can be found all year around.

Prep time: 40 minutes
Servings: 6
Calories per serving: 230

Ingredients:
6 large apples
½ cup walnuts, chopped
¼ cup golden raisins
2 tablespoons dark rum
2 tablespoons agave syrup

Directions:
Carefully remove the core of the apples, leaving them whole and place them all in a deep dish baking pan. Set aside.
In a bowl, mix the walnuts, raisins, dark rum and agave syrup. Spoon the filling into each apple and bake them in the preheated oven at 350F for 30 minutes or until tender and fragrant. Serve them warm with ice cream or chilled with whipped cream.

Fruit Kebabs

These kebabs are a fun way to add fruits into your daily food routine. Kids will surely love their taste, but also getting involved into making them. You can use any fruits you like, just make sure they are as varied as possible.

Prep time: 15 minutes
Servings: 6
Calories per serving: 256

Ingredients:
Kebabs:
2 cups strawberries
1 cup grapes
4 kiwi fruits, peeled and sliced
2 cups melon cubes
6 wooden skewers
Sauce:
½ cup cashew nuts, soaked
½ cup cream cheese
4 tablespoons agave syrup
1 tablespoon lemon juice
1 teaspoon vanilla extract
2 mint leaves, chopped

Directions:
Place the fruits on skewers and arrange them all on a serving platter. Set the kebabs aside.
For the sauce, mix the cashews in a blender until well blended then add the cream cheese, agave syrup, lemon juice and vanilla. Blend until smooth then fold in the chopped mint.
Serve the kebabs dipped into this refreshing sauce.

Key Lime Pie

This is a great way to introduce avocados into your diet. This pie is creamy, delicious and highly refreshing, but the taste is not its only benefit because it is also high in nutrients, such as omega-3 fatty acids and minerals. This pie is the perfect mix between delicious and healthy.

Prep time: 40 minutes
Servings: 10
Calories per serving: 333

Ingredients:
Crust:
1 cup shredded coconut
2/3 cup walnuts
2 teaspoons lime zest
Juice from 1 lime
½ cup dates, pitted
¼ cup coconut milk
Filling:
2 ripe avocados
4 tablespoons lime juice
¼ cup agave syrup
¼ cup coconut oil
2 tablespoons lime zest
1 cup coconut cream

Directions:
To make the crust, mix the coconut, walnuts, lime zest, lime juice, dates and coconut milk in a food processor. Pulse until well blended then transfer the mixture into your pie pan and press it well on the bottom and sides of the pan. Set aside.

For the filling, mix the avocados with the lime juice and zest in a blender. Stir in the agave syrup, coconut oil and coconut cream then spoon the mixture into the crust.

Chia Seed Berry Pudding

This pudding is a delicious and healthy way to start your day on a high note. The chia seeds are known for their high content of nutrients and the berries are a bomb of antioxidants as well. Combined, they create a pudding that can be either a luscious dessert or a healthy breakfast.

Prep time: 10 minutes
Servings: 4
Calories per serving: 97

Ingredients:
¼ cup chia seeds
½ cup water
2 tablespoons agave syrup
2 cups mixed berries
½ teaspoon vanilla extract

Directions:
Bring the water to a boil and stir in the chia seeds. Mix well until the seeds soak all the water. Mix in the agave syrup and vanilla and set aside.
Puree in a blender half of the fruits. Mix the fruits with the chia seeds then stir in the remaining fruits, whole. Serve the pudding fresh.

Apricot Clafoutis

Clafoutis is a French dessert that takes just 5 minutes to mix up and a few more minutes to bake. The final dessert is moist, soft and very similar to a pudding, but delicious and fragrant.

Prep time: 40 minutes
Servings: 8
Calories per serving: 285

Ingredients:
4 apricots, cut in half
1 pinch cinnamon powder
2 cups almond milk
½ cup brown sugar
4 eggs
1 cup rice flour
1 pinch salt

Directions:
Mix the almond milk with the eggs, brown sugar, cinnamon powder, rice flour and salt. Set the batter aside.
Place the apricot halves in a small tart pan. Pour in the batter and bake the clafoutis in the preheated oven at 350F for 35 minutes or until set and golden brown on the edges. Remove from the oven and let it cool down before serving.

Avocado Mint Mousse

There is nothing like an airy, silky avocado mint mousse as dessert. It is the perfect treat for guests, special occasions or just those moments when all you want is to spoil your loved ones. It is an easy to make recipe that yields a fragrant and luscious mousse.

Prep time: 20 minutes
Servings: 6
Calories per serving: 308

Ingredients:
1 ripe avocado
1 teaspoon lime juice
2 tablespoons coconut oil
1 teaspoon vanilla extract
6 mint leaves
2 ½ cups heavy cream
¼ cup powdered sugar

Directions:
Combine the avocado with the lime juice, coconut oil, vanilla and mint in a blender and pulse until smooth. Set aside.
Whip the heavy cream with the powdered sugar then fold it into the avocado mixture. Spoon the mousse into small individual serving glasses and refrigerate 1 hour before serving.

Raspberry Tapioca Pudding

Tapioca is a good source of nutrients, but also a versatile ingredient in the kitchen. This pudding is just one of the possibilities of cooking and combining tapioca. The limit is only your personal taste.

Prep time: 15 minutes
Servings: 6
Calories per serving: 398

Ingredients:
1/3 cup tapioca pearls
3 cups almond milk
½ cup agave syrup
1 teaspoon vanilla extract
1 pinch cardamom
1 cup fresh raspberries

Directions:
Mix the tapioca pearls with the milk and place the saucepan over low to medium heat. Cook for 20-30 minutes, adding the agave syrup, vanilla and cardamom. Spoon the pudding in individual serving glasses and top with raspberries before serving.

Tropical Parfait

The tropical fruits and chia seeds in the recipe create a delicious and silky dessert, perfect for those hot summer days when all you need is a refreshing dessert that takes little time to make but it is at the same time healthy and nutritious.

Prep time: 25 minutes
Servings: 6
Calories per serving: 184

Ingredients:
2 tablespoons chia seeds
1 cup Greek style yogurt
3 tablespoons agave syrup
1 mango, peeled and diced
1 papaya, peeled and diced
1 peach, sliced
½ cup rolled oats

Directions:
Mix the yogurt with the agave syrup and chia seeds. To finish the parfait, start layering the rolled oats with the yogurt and fruits in small individual serving glasses. Refrigerate 1 hour then serve.

Drinks and Treats for Parties

Wild Berry Smoothie

How about a glass of this fragrant and rich smoothie for breakfast? It will surely brighten up your day, while giving you enough nutrients to have enough energy for a long day ahead.

Prep time: 10 minutes
Servings: 4
Calories per serving: 366

Ingredients:
2 cups mixed wild berries, fresh or frozen
2 kale leaves
2 cups almond milk
Juice from ½ lime
2 tablespoons agave syrup

Directions:
Mix all the ingredients in a blender and pulse until well mixed and smooth. Pour in glasses of your choice and serve

Rose Water Fragrant Drink

Made with almond milk and rose water, this drink is fragrant and delightful. The aroma of the rose water will flood your senses and nourish your taste buds. It's a truly special and delicious drink.

Prep time: 10 minutes
Servings: 6
Calories per serving: 398

Ingredients:
3 ½ cups almond milk
½ cup blanched almonds
2 tablespoons rice flour
1 pinch cardamom powder
2 tablespoons agave syrup
2 teaspoons rose water

Directions:
Mix the almond milk with the almonds and rice flour in a blender until smooth. Pour the mixture into a saucepan and cook for 5-10 minutes until it starts to look slightly thicker and creamier. Remove from heat and stir in the agave syrup, cardamom and rose water. Serve it warm or chilled.

Hot Chocolate

What would the cold season be without chocolate?! Hot chocolate is such a versatile drink that has so much richness and such a good taste. Plus, the recipe is incredibly versatile and easily customized to your likings.

Prep time: 15 minutes
Servings: 6
Calories per serving: 432

Ingredients:
¼ cup cocoa powder
¼ cup agave syrup
3 ½ cups almond milk
1 oz. dark chocolate
1 pinch salt
1 pinch cinnamon powder
½ cup heavy cream

Directions:
Mix all the ingredients in a small saucepan and bring to a boil. Cook over medium heat for 5 minutes then pour in cups and serve warm. However, you can serve it when chilled too, topped with a few ice cubes.

White Hot Chocolate

Hot chocolate is a common drink and it is usually made from dark chocolate, but how about a cup of this vanilla flavored white hot chocolate?! It will surprise you with how rich and fragrant it is and it will impress you with its deliciousness and intense aroma.

Prep time: 10 minutes
Servings: 6
Calories per serving: 370

Ingredients:
3 cups almond milk
½ cup white chocolate chips (gluten free)
½ teaspoon vanilla bean paste
1 pinch salt
¼ cup heavy cream

Directions:
Mix the almond milk with the salt and heavy cream and heat them up in a small saucepan. Remove from heat and stir in the white chocolate. Mix until melted then add the vanilla. Pour in cups and serve warm.

Carrot and Pumpkin Smoothie

Raw pumpkin is not only delicious, but also highly nutritious, rich in antioxidants, mainly beta-carotene which we all know how benefic it is for vision and skin. This recipe combines it with fresh carrot juice to create a smoothie that will restore the nutritional balance in your system.

Prep time: 10 minutes
Servings: 4
Calories per serving: 218

Ingredients:
1 cup fresh carrot juice
1 cup fresh orange juice
1 cup pumpkin cubes
1 cup almond milk
½ teaspoon grated ginger
1 pinch nutmeg
1 pinch cinnamon powder
2 tablespoons agave syrup
1 teaspoon lemon juice

Directions:
Mix all the ingredients in a blender and pulse until smooth and creamy. Pour the smoothie in glasses of your choice and serve it as fresh as possible. Feel free to replace the carrot or pumpkin with any other fruit you want.

Chocolate Truffles

These truffles can proudly sit on your party table and bring joy to everyone tasting them. They are creamy, silky and absolutely delicious with their chocolate intense flavor and customizable composition.

Prep time: 30 minutes
Servings: 2 dozen
Calories per serving: 65

Ingredients:
1 cup heavy cream
1 cup dark chocolate chips
2 tablespoons honey
2 tablespoons butter
1 pinch salt
1 teaspoon orange zest
¼ cup cocoa powder to coat

Directions:
Bring the heavy cream to the boiling point then remove from heat and stir in the chocolate and honey. Mix until melted then add the butter, salt and orange zest. Mix well then refrigerate the mixture for 1 hour to set. From small balls from the mixture and roll each ball into cocoa powder. Serve them right away.

Peanut Butter Popcorn Truffles

Although slightly unusual, these truffles combine the crunchy popcorn with peanut butter and chocolate, creating some great snacks for your party. Everyone will love these bitter sweet little truffles.

Prep time: 1 hour
Servings: 2 dozen
Calories per serving: 122

Ingredients:
2 cups popcorn
¼ cup rolled oats
½ cup peanut butter
2 tablespoons agave syrup
2 tablespoons butter
8 oz. dark chocolate, melted

Directions:
Mix the peanut butter with the agave syrup and butter and melt them together over low heat. Pour the mixture over the popcorn and stir in the oats too. Mix very well then form small balls of mixture. Place them all on a baking sheet and freeze for 15 minutes. After 15 minutes, roll each ball into melted chocolate and refrigerate them all 10 minutes to set before serving.

Chocolate Dipped Candied Orange Peel

I love snacks that are easy to make and quick, but don't make any sacrifice in terms of taste and texture and these dipped candied peels are the perfect example of such dessert because they combine the amazing flavor of the orange peel with the bittersweet taste of the chocolate coating.

Prep time: 50 minutes
Servings: 2 dozen
Calories per serving: 88

Ingredients:
1 cup sugar, plus extra for rolling
3 organic oranges
1 ½ cups water
5 oz. dark chocolate, melted

Directions:
Carefully remove the peel from all 3 oranges and slice it finely. Place the peel in a saucepan and cover it with water. Bring it to a boil then remove from heat and strain. Pour water again, just enough to cover the peel and repeat the same process one more time. This task is made to remove the bitter taste of the orange peel. Strain and set aside.
Combine the sugar with the water and boil for 2 minutes then add the peel and cook for 10 minutes or more. Add more water if it starts to get thick. The final peel should be soft and the syrup should be quite thick. Remove the peel from the syrup and quickly roll all the strips through granulated sugar.
Dip each peel strip into melted chocolate and let them set on a baking sheet.

Mocha Fudge

Who wouldn't love a piece of fudge when at a party? Especially if it is a fudge that combines the flavor of chocolate with coffee and caramel. It can't get better than this because this fudge melts in your mouth bite after bite and leaves wanting more.

Prep time: 30 minutes
Servings: 18
Calories per serving: 189

Ingredients:
1 ½ cups hot water
4 teaspoons instant coffee
1 ½ cups milk
3 cups sugar
¼ cup butter
1 cup dark chocolate chips
1 pinch salt

Directions:
Mix the hot water with the instant coffee, then add the milk, sugar, butter and chocolate. Place the saucepan over medium heat and cook for 20 minutes until it thickens. Pour the mixture into a small baking pan lined with plastic wrap and refrigerate for 2 hours. Cut into small squares and serve.

Peanut Butter Brownies

I sure love a square of brownies anywhere I got and even more at a party because they can easily be grabbed on the run without being messy, but at the same time being delicious and moist.

Prep time: 40 minutes
Servings: 12
Calories per serving: 318

Ingredients:
½ cup vegetable oil
1 cup peanut butter
¼ cup brown sugar
¼ cup agave syrup
3 eggs
1 cup almond flour
¼ cup cocoa powder
2 tablespoons flax seeds, ground
1 pinch salt

Directions:
Mix the oil with the peanut butter, brown sugar, agave syrup and eggs. Stir in the almond flour, cocoa powder, flax seeds and salt. Mix well then pour the batter into small baking pan lined with parchment paper. Bake in the preheated oven at 350F for 30 minutes. When done, let them cool in the pan then cut them into small squares.

Conclusion

Food allergies and intolerances are not easy to deal with given all the variety of food available on the market, food that often comes with a nice presentation and tempts even the pickiest eaters. But you don't have to give up on your favorite foods just because you have an allergy either and desserts don't fall under the forbidden category, even when you're not allowed gluten!

Yes, it is true, most desserts contain plenty of gluten, but there are plenty of non-gluten options too and even though the making process and the ingredient list is different, the recipes are designed so that the final taste is just as good as traditionally baked sweets.

Next time you go shopping, stock up on gluten free baking ingredients and mix your way to a delightful life and an enjoyable dessert moment because you can now indulge on desserts too, despite your allergy. It is easy, delicious and healthy. What more can you ask for?

Thanks for reading!

A lot of love and care went into putting together these recipes and I do hope you enjoyed the book.

If you did, you could help support me most of all with an honest review on Amazon!

You would really make my day!

Simply head to Amazon.com and click *Your Account* followed by *Your Orders* to locate the book.

44468751R10044

Made in the USA
Middletown, DE
07 May 2019